The Far Side®

Just Plain STUPID!

2 0 0 3 Desk Calendar

Gary Larson

Andrews McMeel Publishing

an Andrews McMeel Universal company
Kansas City

www.andrewsmcmeel.com

ISBN: 0-7407-2384-7

Perhaps the scientist in the well known Far Side cartoon said it best when he remarked, "It's time we face reality, my friends. ... We're not exactly rocket scientists." To be sure, many of the characters in Gary Larson's cartoons often have, over the years, exhibited a level of intelligence somewhat less than, say, the average phone psychic patron ("The charge is $7.95 a minute, will you hold, please?"). In fact, the history of The Far Side® is littered with instances of kids pushing doors clearly marked "pull," of cows perched on electric fences, and of dinosaurs with brains "about the size of a walnut." For this calendar, we've delved to the depths of that great mine of stupidity and emerged with no fewer than fifty-three gleaming nuggets of downright dumbness. Not only will you be amused throughout the year, you'll also feel darn smart for having the good sense to buy this calendar (instead of, perhaps, a Psychic Pals phone card).

JAnUary 2003

Sunday	Monday	Tuesday	Wednesday	Thursday	Friday	Saturday
29 *December 2002*	30	31	1 New Year's Day Kwanzaa ends (USA)	2 Day after New Year's Day (NZ) Bank Holiday (Scotland)	3	4
5	6	7	8	9	10	11
12	13	14	15	16	17	18
19	20 Martin Luther King Jr.'s Birthday (observed) (USA)	21	22	23	24	25
26	27 Australia Day (observed)	28	29	30	31	1

DeCembeR 2002

S	M	T	W	T	F	S
1	2	3	4	5	6	7
8	9	10	11	12	13	14
15	16	17	18	19	20	21
22	23	24	25	26	27	28
29	30	31				

FebRuarY 2003

S	M	T	W	T	F	S
						1
2	3	4	5	6	7	8
9	10	11	12	13	14	15
16	17	18	19	20	21	22
23	24	25	26	27	28	

Notes

"Oh, what a cute little Siamese. ... Is he friendly?"

DeC 2002- JAn 2003

_____
_____
_____
_____
_____
_____
_____
_____
_____
_____
_____
_____
_____
_____
_____
_____

Monday
30

Tuesday
31

New Year's Day
Kwanzaa ends (USA)

Wednesday
1

Day after New Year's Day (NZ)
Bank Holiday (Scotland)

Thursday
2

Friday
3

Saturday
4

Sunday
5

JAnUary 2003

S	M	T	W	T	F	S
			1	2	3	4
5	6	7	8	9	10	11
12	13	14	15	16	17	18
19	20	21	22	23	24	25
26	27	28	29	30	31	

"Hey! You! ... No cutting in!"

JAnUary 2003

Monday
6

Tuesday
7

Wednesday
8

Thursday
9

Friday
10

Saturday
11

Sunday
12

JAnUary 2003

S	M	T	W	T	F	S
			1	2	3	4
5	6	7	8	9	10	11
12	13	14	15	16	17	18
19	20	21	22	23	24	25
26	27	28	29	30	31	

"Now this next slide, gentlemen, demonstrates the awesome power of our twenty megaton ... for crying-out-loud! Not again!"

JAnUAry
2003

Monday

13

Tuesday

14

Wednesday

15

Thursday

16

Friday

17

Saturday

18

Sunday

19

JAnUary 2003

S	M	T	W	T	F	S
			1	2	3	4
5	6	7	8	9	10	11
12	13	14	15	16	17	18
19	20	21	22	23	24	25
26	27	28	29	30	31	

"Bob! You fool! Don't plug that thing in!"

January
2003

Monday
20
Martin Luther King Jr.'s Birthday (observed) (USA)

Tuesday
21

Wednesday
22

Thursday
23

Friday
24

Saturday
25

Sunday
26

January 2003

S	M	T	W	T	F	S
			1	2	3	4
5	6	7	8	9	10	11
12	13	14	15	16	17	18
19	20	21	22	23	24	25
26	27	28	29	30	31	

FebRuary 2003

Sunday	Monday	Tuesday	Wednesday	Thursday	Friday	Saturday
26	27	28	29	30	31	1
2 Groundhog Day (USA)	3	4	5	6 Waitangi Day (NZ)	7	8
9	10	11	12	13	14 St. Valentine's Day	15
16	17 Presidents' Day (USA)	18	19	20	21	22
23	24	25	26	27	28	1

JAnUary 2003

S	M	T	W	T	F	S
			1	2	3	4
5	6	7	8	9	10	11
12	13	14	15	16	17	18
19	20	21	22	23	24	25
26	27	28	29	30	31	

MArcH 2003

S	M	T	W	T	F	S
						1
2	3	4	5	6	7	8
9	10	11	12	13	14	15
16	17	18	19	20	21	22
23/30	24/31	25	26	27	28	29

Notes

"We're almost free, everyone! I just felt the first drop of rain!"

JAn-Feb 2003

Australia Day (observed)

Monday 27

Tuesday 28

Wednesday 29

Thursday 30

Friday 31

Saturday 1

Groundhog Day (USA)

Sunday 2

FebRuary 2003

S	M	T	W	T	F	S
						1
2	3	4	5	6	7	8
9	10	11	12	13	14	15
16	17	18	19	20	21	22
23	24	25	26	27	28	

"The fuel light's on, Frank! We're all going to die! ... Wait, wait. ...
Oh, my mistake—that's the intercom light."

FebRuary 2003

Monday

3

Tuesday

4

Wednesday

5

Waitangi Day (NZ)

Thursday

6

Friday

7

Saturday

8

Sunday

9

FebRuary 2003

S	M	T	W	T	F	S
						1
2	3	4	5	6	7	8
9	10	11	12	13	14	15
16	17	18	19	20	21	22
23	24	25	26	27	28	

FebRuary
2003

_____
_____
_____
_____
_____
_____
_____
_____
_____
_____
_____
_____
_____
_____
_____
_____
_____
_____
_____
_____
_____
_____

FebRuary 2003

S	M	T	W	T	F	S
						1
2	3	4	5	6	7	8
9	10	11	12	13	14	15
16	17	18	19	20	21	22
23	24	25	26	27	28	

Monday
10

Tuesday
11

Wednesday
12

Thursday
13

St. Valentine's Day

Friday
14

Saturday
15

Sunday
16

"And the murderer is … THE BUTLER! Yes, the butler—
who, I'm convinced, first gored the Colonel to death
before trampling him to smithereens."

FebRuary 2003

Presidents' Day (USA)

Monday
17

Tuesday
18

Wednesday
19

Thursday
20

Friday
21

Saturday
22

Sunday
23

FebRuary 2003

S	M	T	W	T	F	S
						1
2	3	4	5	6	7	8
9	10	11	12	13	14	15
16	17	18	19	20	21	22
23	24	25	26	27	28	

MArcH 2003

Sunday	Monday	Tuesday	Wednesday	Thursday	Friday	Saturday
23	24	25	26	27	28	1 St. David's Day (UK)
2	3 Labour Day (Australia—WA) Eight Hours Day (Australia—TAS)	4	5 Ash Wednesday	6	7	8 International Women's Day
9	10 Labour Day (Australia—VIC) Canberra Day (Australia—ACT) Commonwealth Day (Australia, NZ, UK)	11	12	13	14	15
16	17 St. Patrick's Day	18 Purim	19	20	21	22
23 30 Mothering Sunday (UK)	24 31	25	26	27	28	29

FebRuarY 2003

S	M	T	W	T	F	S
						1
2	3	4	5	6	7	8
9	10	11	12	13	14	15
16	17	18	19	20	21	22
23	24	25	26	27	28	

ApRil 2003

S	M	T	W	T	F	S
		1	2	3	4	5
6	7	8	9	10	11	12
13	14	15	16	17	18	19
20	21	22	23	24	25	26
27	28	29	30			

Notes

"Don't be 'fraid, Dug. Me teach him sit on finger. ... Closer, Dug, closer."

Feb-MAr 2003

Monday
24

Tuesday
25

Wednesday
26

Thursday
27

Friday
28

St. David's Day (UK)

Saturday
1

Sunday
2

MARCH 2003

S	M	T	W	T	F	S
						1
2	3	4	5	6	7	8
9	10	11	12	13	14	15
16	17	18	19	20	21	22
23	24	25	26	27	28	29
30	31					

"How many times did I say it, Harold? How many times?
'Make sure that bomb shelter's got a can opener—
ain't much good without a can opener,' I said."

MArcH
2003

_____

_____

_____

_____

_____

_____

_____

_____

_____

_____

_____

_____

_____

_____

_____

_____

_____

_____

_____

_____

MArcH 2003

S	M	T	W	T	F	S
						I
2	3	4	5	6	7	8
9	10	11	12	13	14	15
16	17	18	19	20	21	22
23	24	25	26	27	28	29
30	31					

Labour Day (Australia—WA)
Eight Hours Day (Australia—TAS)

Monday

3

Tuesday

4

Ash Wednesday

Wednesday

5

Thursday

6

Friday

7

International Women's Day

Saturday

8

Sunday

9

School for the mechanically declined

MArcH
2003

Monday
IO

Tuesday
II

Wednesday
I2

Thursday
I3

Friday
I4

Saturday
I5

Sunday
I6

MArcH 2003

S	M	T	W	T	F	S
						I
2	3	4	5	6	7	8
9	IO	II	I2	I3	I4	I5
I6	I7	I8	I9	20	2I	22
23	24	25	26	27	28	29
30	3I					

"Hang him, you idiots! Hang him! ...
'String-him-up' is a figure of speech!"

MArcH
2003

_____

_____

_____

_____

_____

_____

_____

_____

_____

_____

_____

_____

_____

_____

_____

_____

_____

_____

_____

_____

_____

MArcH 2003

S	M	T	W	T	F	S
						I
2	3	4	5	6	7	8
9	10	11	12	13	14	15
16	17	18	19	20	21	22
23	24	25	26	27	28	29
30	31					

Mothering Sunday (UK

MArcH
2003

_____

_____

_____

_____

_____

_____

_____

_____

_____

_____

_____

_____

_____

_____

_____

_____

_____

_____

MArcH 2003

S	M	T	W	T	F	S
						I
2	3	4	5	6	7	8
9	10	11	12	13	14	15
16	17	18	19	20	21	22
23	24	25	26	27	28	29
30	31					

St. Patrick's Day | Monday
17

Purim | Tuesday
18

Wednesday
19

Thursday
20

Friday
21

Saturday
22

Sunday
23

"Look, if it was elect..."

April 2003

Sunday	Monday	Tuesday	Wednesday	Thursday	Friday	Saturday
30	31	1	2	3	4	5
6	7	8	9	10	11	12
13 Palm Sunday	14 Bank Holiday (Australia—TAS)	15	16	17 First Day of Passover	18 Good Friday (Western)	19 Easter Saturday (Australia—except VIC, WA)
20 Easter Sunday (Western)	21 Easter Monday (Australia, Canada, NZ, UK—except Scotland)	22 Earth Day	23 St. George's Day (UK)	24 Last Day of Passover	25 Anzac Day (Australia, NZ) Good Friday (Orthodox)	26
27 Easter Sunday (Orthodox)	28	29	30	1	2	3

March 2003

S	M	T	W	T	F	S
						1
2	3	4	5	6	7	8
9	10	11	12	13	14	15
16	17	18	19	20	21	22
23/30	24/31	25	26	27	28	29

May 2003

S	M	T	W	T	F	S
				1	2	3
4	5	6	7	8	9	10
11	12	13	14	15	16	17
18	19	20	21	22	23	24
25	26	27	28	29	30	31

Notes

Misunderstanding his dying father's advice,
Arnie spent several years protecting the family mules.

April 2003

	Monday
	7

	Tuesday
	8

	Wednesday
	9

	Thursday
	10

	Friday
	11

	Saturday
	12

Palm Sunday	Sunday
	13

April 2003

S	M	T	W	T	F	S
		1	2	3	4	5
6	7	8	9	10	11	12
13	14	15	16	17	18	19
20	21	22	23	24	25	26
27	28	29	30			

"So, Andre! ... The king wants to know how
you're coming with 'St. George and the Dragon.'"

April 2003

Easter Monday (Australia, Canada, NZ, UK—except Scotland)

Monday
21

Earth Day

Tuesday
22

St. George's Day (UK)

Wednesday
23

Last Day of Passover

Thursday
24

Anzac Day (Australia, NZ)
Good Friday (Orthodox)

Friday
25

Saturday
26

Easter Sunday (Orthodox)

Sunday
27

April 2003

S	M	T	W	T	F	S
		1	2	3	4	5
6	7	8	9	10	11	12
13	14	15	16	17	18	19
20	21	22	23	24	25	26
27	28	29	30			

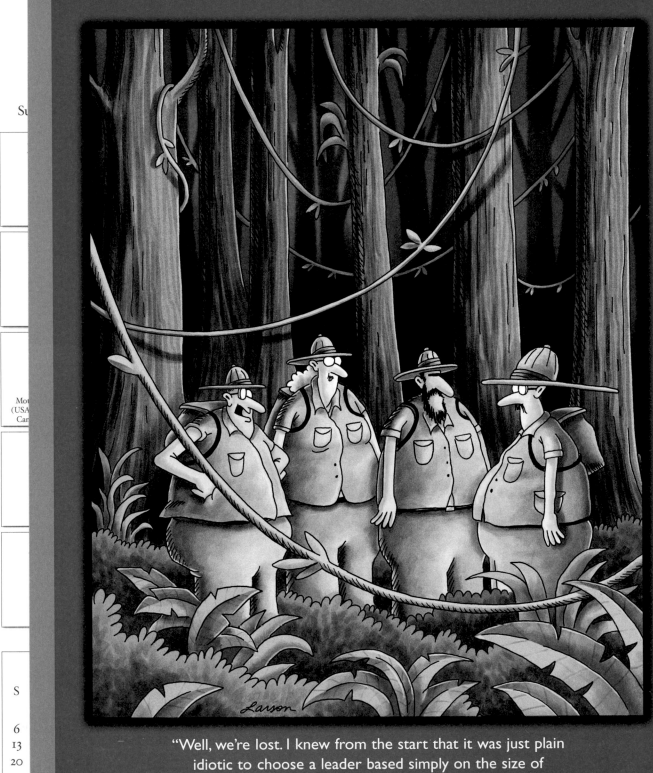

"Well, we're lost. I knew from the start that it was just plain idiotic to choose a leader based simply on the size of his or her respective pith helmet. Sorry, Cromwell."

MAY 2003

Labour Day (Australia – QLD)
Bank Holiday (Eire, UK)

Mother's Day (USA, Australia, Canada, NZ)

May 2003

S	M	T	W	T	F	S
				1	2	3
4	5	6	7	8	9	10
11	12	13	14	15	16	17
18	19	20	21	22	23	24
25	26	27	28	29	30	31

APR-MAY 2003

Monday
28

Tuesday
29

Wednesday
30

Thursday
1

Friday
2

Saturday
3

Sunday
4

May 2003

S	M	T	W	T	F	S
				1	2	3
4	5	6	7	8	9	10
11	12	13	14	15	16	17
18	19	20	21	22	23	24
25	26	27	28	29	30	31

"Eddie! I've told you a hundred times
never to run with that through the house!"

"I'm sorry, Delores, but I didn't think you'd truly ever leave! ...
But where will you go?"

May
2003

Monday
12

Tuesday
13

Wednesday
14

Thursday
15

Friday
16

Armed Forces Day (USA)

Saturday
17

Sunday
18

May 2003

S	M	T	W	T	F	S
				1	2	3
4	5	6	7	8	9	10
11	12	13	14	15	16	17
18	19	20	21	22	23	24
25	26	27	28	29	30	31

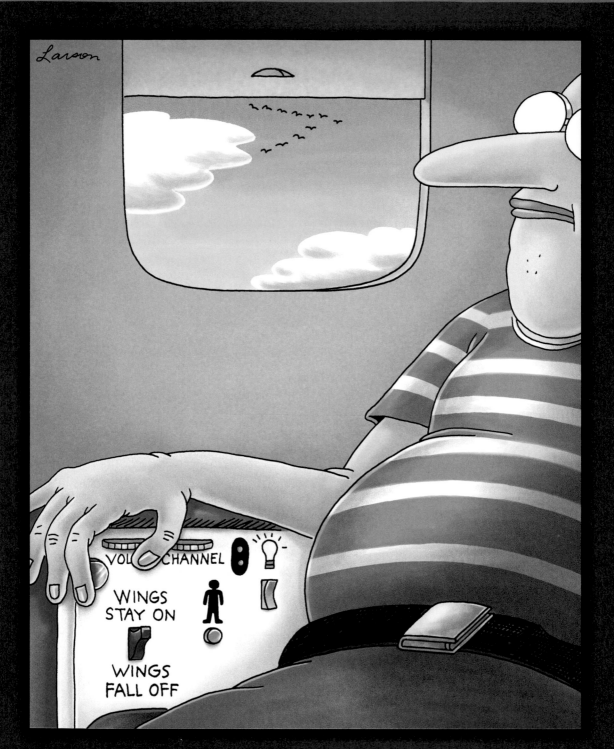

Fumbling for his recline button, Ted unwittingly instigates a disaster.

May
2003

Monday
19

Tuesday
20

Wednesday
21

Thursday
22

Friday
23

Saturday
24

Sunday
25

May 2003

S	M	T	W	T	F	S
				1	2	3
4	5	6	7	8	9	10
11	12	13	14	15	16	17
18	19	20	21	22	23	24
25	26	27	28	29	30	31

June 2003

Sunday	Monday	Tuesday	Wednesday	Thursday	Friday	Saturday
1	2 Queen's Birthday (NZ) Foundation Day (Australia—WA) Bank Holiday (Eire)	3	4	5	6 Shavuot begins	7 Shavuot ends
8 Whitsunday	9 Queen's Birthday (Australia—except WA)	10	11	12	13	14 Flag Day (USA)
15 Father's Day (USA, Canada, UK)	16	17	18	19 Corpus Christi	20	21
22	23	24	25	26	27	28
29	30	1	2	3	4	5

May 2003

S	M	T	W	T	F	S
				1	2	3
4	5	6	7	8	9	10
11	12	13	14	15	16	17
18	19	20	21	22	23	24
25	26	27	28	29	30	31

July 2003

S	M	T	W	T	F	S
		1	2	3	4	5
6	7	8	9	10	11	12
13	14	15	16	17	18	19
20	21	22	23	24	25	26
27	28	29	30	31		

Notes

S	M	
1	2	1
8	9	10
15	16	17
22	23	
29	30	

JuNe 2003

Monday
2

Tuesday
3

Wednesday
4

Thursday
5

Shavuot begins

Friday
6

Shavuot ends

Saturday
7

Whitsunday

Sunday
8

JuNe 2003

S	M	T	W	T	F	S
1	2	3	4	5	6	7
8	9	10	11	12	13	14
15	16	17	18	19	20	21
22	23	24	25	26	27	28
29	30					

"Oh, this should be interesting. ... Looks as if your father has forgotten about the phenomenon of windows again."

JuNe 2003

Queen's Birthday (Australia—except WA)

Monday
9

Tuesday
IO

Wednesday
II

Thursday
I2

Friday
I3

Flag Day (USA)

Saturday
I4

Father's Day (USA, Canada, UK)

Sunday
I5

JuNe 2003

S	M	T	W	T	F	S
I	2	3	4	5	6	7
8	9	IO	II	I2	I3	I4
I5	I6	I7	I8	I9	20	2I
22	23	24	25	26	27	28
29	30					

Inadvertently, Roy dooms the entire earth to annihilation when,
in an attempt to be friendly, he seizes their leader
by the head and shakes vigorously.

JuNe 2003

Monday
16

Tuesday
17

Wednesday
18

Corpus Christi

Thursday
19

Friday
20

Saturday
21

Sunday
22

JuNe 2003

S	M	T	W	T	F	S
1	2	3	4	5	6	7
8	9	10	11	12	13	14
15	16	17	18	19	20	21
22	23	24	25	26	27	28
29	30					

JuLy 2003

Sunday	Monday	Tuesday	Wednesday	Thursday	Friday	Saturday
29	30	1 Canada Day	2	3	4 Independence Day (USA)	5
6	7	8	9	10	11	12 Battle of the Boyne Day (Northern Ireland)
13	14	15	16	17	18	19
20	21	22	23	24	25	26
27	28	29	30	31	1	2

JuNe 2003

S	M	T	W	T	F	S
1	2	3	4	5	6	7
8	9	10	11	12	13	14
15	16	17	18	19	20	21
22	23	24	25	26	27	28
29	30					

AUguSt 2003

S	M	T	W	T	F	S
					1	2
3	4	5	6	7	8	9
10	11	12	13	14	15	16
17	18	19	20	21	22	23
24/31	25	26	27	28	29	30

Notes

"Here are the blueprints. Now look: This is going to be the *Liberty* Bell, so we obviously expect that it be forged with great diligence and skill."

JuNe-JuLy 2003

Monday

30

Canada Day

Tuesday

1

Wednesday

2

Thursday

3

Independence Day (USA)

Friday

4

Saturday

5

Sunday

6

JuLy 2003

S	M	T	W	T	F	S
		1	2	3	4	5
6	7	8	9	10	11	12
13	14	15	16	17	18	19
20	21	22	23	24	25	26
27	28	29	30	31		

Never, never do this.

JuLy 2003

Monday
7

Tuesday
8

Wednesday
9

Thursday
IO

Friday
II

Battle of the Boyne Day (Northern Ireland)

Saturday
I2

Sunday
I3

JuLy 2003

S	M	T	W	T	F	S
		I	2	3	4	5
6	7	8	9	IO	II	I2
I3	I4	I5	I6	I7	I8	I9
20	2I	22	23	24	25	26
27	28	29	30	3I		

"For heaven's sake, Elroy! *Now* look where the earth is! ...
Move over and let me drive!"

JuLy
2003

Monday
14

Tuesday
15

Wednesday
16

Thursday
17

Friday
18

Saturday
19

Sunday
20

JuLy 2003

S	M	T	W	T	F	S
		1	2	3	4	5
6	7	8	9	10	11	12
13	14	15	16	17	18	19
20	21	22	23	24	25	26
27	28	29	30	31		

Stupid birds

JuLy 2003

Monday

21

Tuesday

22

Wednesday

23

Thursday

24

Friday

25

Saturday

26

Sunday

27

JuLy 2003

S	M	T	W	T	F	S
		1	2	3	4	5
6	7	8	9	10	11	12
13	14	15	16	17	18	19
20	21	22	23	24	25	26
27	28	29	30	31		

AUguSt 2003

Sunday	Monday	Tuesday	Wednesday	Thursday	Friday	Saturday
27	28	29	30	31	1	2
3	4 Bank Holiday (Australia—NSW, ACT, Eire, Scotland) Picnic Day (Australia—NT)	5	6	7	8	9
10	11	12	13	14	15 Assumption	16
17	18	19	20	21	22	23
24 / 31	25 Bank Holiday (UK—except Scotland)	26	27	28	29	30

JuLy 2003

S	M	T	W	T	F	S
		1	2	3	4	5
6	7	8	9	10	11	12
13	14	15	16	17	18	19
20	21	22	23	24	25	26
27	28	29	30	31		

September 2003

S	M	T	W	T	F	S
	1	2	3	4	5	6
7	8	9	10	11	12	13
14	15	16	17	18	19	20
21	22	23	24	25	26	27
28	29	30				

Notes

"Matthews ... we're getting another one of those
strange 'aw blah es span yol' sounds."

JuLy-AUg
2003

Monday

28

Tuesday

29

Wednesday

30

Thursday

31

Friday

1

Saturday

2

Sunday

3

AUguSt 2003

S	M	T	W	T	F	S
					1	2
3	4	5	6	7	8	9
10	11	12	13	14	15	16
17	18	19	20	21	22	23
24	25	26	27	28	29	30
31						

"Uh-oh ... I've got a feeling I shouldn't have been munching on these things for the last mile."

AUgUSt
2003

Bank Holiday (Australia—NSW, ACT, Eire, Scotland)
Picnic Day (Australia—NT)

Monday

4

Tucsday

5

Wednesday

6

Thursday

7

Friday

8

Saturday

9

Sunday

10

AUgUSt 2003

S	M	T	W	T	F	S
					1	2
3	4	5	6	7	8	9
10	11	12	13	14	15	16
17	18	19	20	21	22	23
24	25	26	27	28	29	30
31						

Dumb ox

AUguSt 2003

Monday

11

Tuesday

12

Wednesday

13

Thursday

14

Assumption

Friday

15

Saturday

16

Sunday

17

AUguSt 2003

S	M	T	W	T	F	S
					1	2
3	4	5	6	7	8	9
10	11	12	13	14	15	16
17	18	19	20	21	22	23
24	25	26	27	28	29	30
31						

Animal nerds

AUGUST
2003

Monday
18

Tuesday
19

Wednesday
20

Thursday
21

Friday
22

Saturday
23

Sunday
24

August 2003

S	M	T	W	T	F	S
					1	2
3	4	5	6	7	8	9
10	11	12	13	14	15	16
17	18	19	20	21	22	23
24	25	26	27	28	29	30
31						

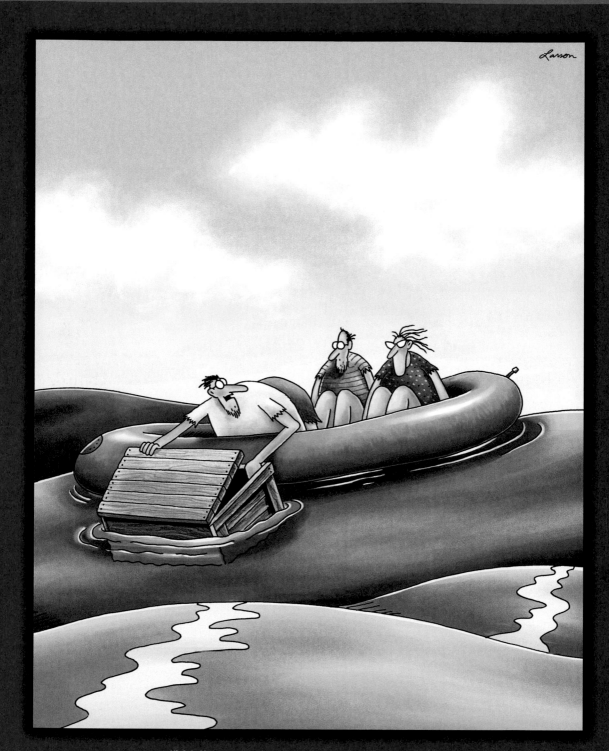

"Well, we might as well put it on board—
although I'm not sure what use we'll have for
a box of rusty nails, broken glass, and throwing darts."

AUguSt 2003

Bank Holiday (UK—except Scotland)

Monday
25

Tuesday
26

Wednesday
27

Thursday
28

Friday
29

Saturday
30

Sunday
31

AUguSt 2003

S	M	T	W	T	F	S
					1	2
3	4	5	6	7	8	9
10	11	12	13	14	15	16
17	18	19	20	21	22	23
24	25	26	27	28	29	30
31						

Her answer off by miles, Sheila's "cow sense"
was always a target of ridicule.

September 2003

Labor Day (USA, Canada)

Monday

1

Tuesday

2

Wednesday

3

Thursday

4

Friday

5

Saturday

6

Father's Day (Australia, NZ)

Sunday

7

September 2003

S	M	T	W	T	F	S
	1	2	3	4	5	6
7	8	9	10	11	12	13
14	15	16	17	18	19	20
21	22	23	24	25	26	27
28	29	30				

"Shhhh, Zog! ... Here come one now!"

September 2003

Monday
8

Tuesday
9

Wednesday
10

Thursday
11

Friday
12

Saturday
13

Sunday
14

September 2003

S	M	T	W	T	F	S
	1	2	3	4	5	6
7	8	9	10	11	12	13
14	15	16	17	18	19	20
21	22	23	24	25	26	27
28	29	30				

"FLETCHER, YOU FOOL! ... THE GATE! THE GATE!"

SeptembeR 2003

_____

_____

_____

_____

_____

_____

_____

_____

_____

_____

_____

_____

_____

_____

_____

_____

_____

_____

_____

SeptembeR 2003

S	M	T	W	T	F	S
	1	2	3	4	5	6
7	8	9	10	11	12	13
14	15	16	17	18	19	20
21	22	23	24	25	26	27
28	29	30				

Monday
15

Tuesday
16

Wednesday
17

Thursday
18

Friday
19

Saturday
20

Sunday
21

September 2003

	Monday
	22

	Tuesday
	23

	Wednesday
	24

	Thursday
	25

	Friday
	26

Rosh Hashanah begins	Saturday
	27

Rosh Hashanah ends	Sunday
	28

September 2003

S	M	T	W	T	F	S
	1	2	3	4	5	6
7	8	9	10	11	12	13
14	15	16	17	18	19	20
21	22	23	24	25	26	27
28	29	30				

October 2003

Sunday	Monday	Tuesday	Wednesday	Thursday	Friday	Saturday
28	29	30	1	2	3	4
5	6 Yom Kippur Labour Day (Australia—ACT, NSW, SA)	7	8	9	10	11 First Day of Tabernacles
12 Second Day of Tabernacles	13 Columbus Day (USA) Thanksgiving (Canada)	14	15	16	17	18
19	20	21	22	23	24 United Nations Day	25
26	27 Labour Day (NZ) Bank Holiday (Eire)	28	29	30	31 Halloween	1

September 2003

S	M	T	W	T	F	S
	1	2	3	4	5	6
7	8	9	10	11	12	13
14	15	16	17	18	19	20
21	22	23	24	25	26	27
28	29	30				

November 2003

S	M	T	W	T	F	S
						1
2	3	4	5	6	7	8
9	10	11	12	13	14	15
16	17	18	19	20	21	22
23/30	24	25	26	27	28	29

Notes

"Well, we're lost ... and it's probably just a matter of time
before someone decides to shoot us."

SEPt-Oct 2003

Queen's Birthday (Australia—WA)

Monday
29

Tuesday
30

Wednesday
1

Thursday
2

Friday
3

Saturday
4

Sunday
5

OctoBeR 2003

S	M	T	W	T	F	S
			1	2	3	4
5	6	7	8	9	10	11
12	13	14	15	16	17	18
19	20	21	22	23	24	25
26	27	28	29	30	31	

People who don't know which end is up

OctoBeR 2003

_____
_____
_____
_____
_____
_____
_____
_____
_____
_____
_____
_____
_____
_____
_____
_____
_____
_____
_____
_____

OctoBeR 2003

S	M	T	W	T	F	S
			1	2	3	4
5	6	7	8	9	10	11
12	13	14	15	16	17	18
19	20	21	22	23	24	25
26	27	28	29	30	31	

Yom Kippur
Labour Day (Australia—ACT, NSW, SA)

Monday
6

Tuesday
7

Wednesday
8

Thursday
9

Friday
10

First Day of Tabernacles

Saturday
11

Second Day of Tabernacles

Sunday
12

"Open the gate! It's a big weiner dog!"

OctoBeR 2003

_____
_____
_____
_____
_____
_____
_____
_____
_____
_____
_____
_____
_____
_____
_____
_____
_____

OctoBeR 2003

S	M	T	W	T	F	S
			1	2	3	4
5	6	7	8	9	10	11
12	13	14	15	16	17	18
19	20	21	22	23	24	25
26	27	28	29	30	31	

Columbus Day (USA)
Thanksgiving (Canada)

Monday
13

Tuesday
14

Wednesday
15

Thursday
16

Friday
17

Saturday
18

Sunday
19

"Shoot! You not only got the wrong planet, you got the wrong *solar* system! ... I mean, a wrong planet I can understand—but a whole solar system?"

OctoBeR 2003

_____
_____
_____
_____
_____
_____
_____
_____
_____
_____
_____
_____
_____
_____
_____
_____
_____
_____
_____
_____
_____
_____
_____

OctoBeR 2003

S	M	T	W	T	F	S
			1	2	3	4
5	6	7	8	9	10	11
12	13	14	15	16	17	18
19	20	21	22	23	24	25
26	27	28	29	30	31	

Monday
20

Tuesday
21

Wednesday
22

Thursday
23

United Nations Day   Friday
24

Saturday
25

Sunday
26

NoVemBeR 2003

Sunday	Monday	Tuesday	Wednesday	Thursday	Friday	Saturday
26	27	28	29	30	31	1 All Saints' Day
2 All Souls' Day	3	4 Election Day (USA)	5	6	7	8
9	10	11 Veterans' Day (USA) Remembrance Day (Canada, UK)	12	13	14	15
16	17	18	19	20	21	22
23 30 St. Andrew's Day (UK)	24	25	26	27 Thanksgiving (USA)	28	29

OctoBeR 2003

S	M	T	W	T	F	S
			1	2	3	4
5	6	7	8	9	10	11
12	13	14	15	16	17	18
19	20	21	22	23	24	25
26	27	28	29	30	31	

DeCembeR 2003

S	M	T	W	T	F	S
	1	2	3	4	5	6
7	8	9	10	11	12	13
14	15	16	17	18	19	20
21	22	23	24	25	26	27
28	29	30	31			

Notes

"Curses! ... How long does it take Igor to go out
and bring back a simple little brain, anyway?"

Oct-Nov 2003

Labour Day (NZ)
Bank Holiday (Eire)

Tuesday

28

Wednesday

29

Thursday

30

Halloween

Friday

31

All Saints' Day

Saturday

1

All Souls' Day

Sunday

2

November 2003

S	M	T	W	T	F	S
						1
2	3	4	5	6	7	8
9	10	11	12	13	14	15
16	17	18	19	20	21	22
23	24	25	26	27	28	29
30						

Math anxiety

Latin convulsions

Chemistry conniptions

Physics floundering

Wood shop apathy

Basic stupidity

Classroom afflictions

NoVemBeR 2003

Monday

3

Election Day (USA)

Tuesday

4

Wednesday

5

Thursday

6

Friday

7

Saturday

8

Sunday

9

NoVemBeR 2003

S	M	T	W	T	F	S
						1
2	3	4	5	6	7	8
9	10	11	12	13	14	15
16	17	18	19	20	21	22
23	24	25	26	27	28	29
30						

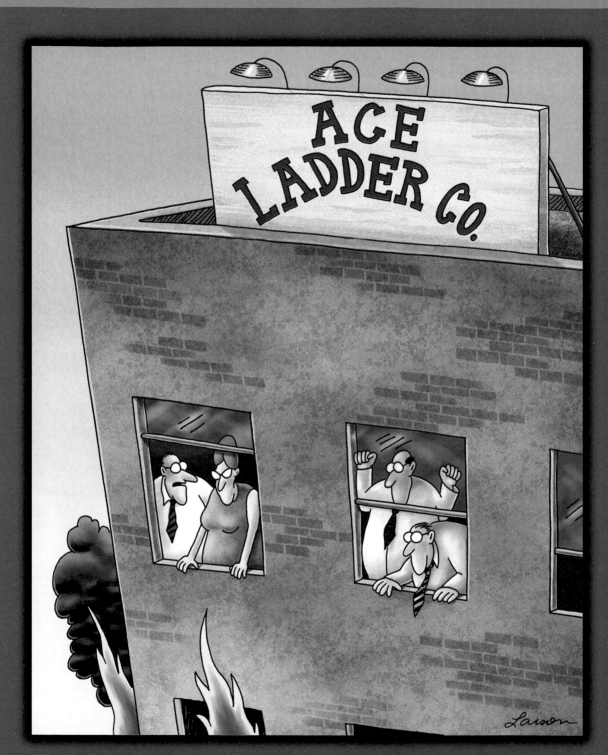

"Wait a minute! Say that again, Doris! ...
You know, the part about 'If only we had some means of climbing down.'"

NoVeMBeR 2003

Monday
10

Tuesday
11

Veterans' Day (USA)
Remembrance Day (Canada, UK)

Wednesday
12

Thursday
13

Friday
14

Saturday
15

Sunday
16

NoVeMBeR 2003

S	M	T	W	T	F	S
						1
2	3	4	5	6	7	8
9	10	11	12	13	14	15
16	17	18	19	20	21	22
23	24	25	26	27	28	29
30						

And no one ever heard from the Anderson brothers again.

NoVemBeR 2003

Monday

17

Tuesday

18

Wednesday

19

Thursday

20

Friday

21

Saturday

22

Sunday

23

NoVemBeR 2003

S	M	T	W	T	F	S
						1
2	3	4	5	6	7	8
9	10	11	12	13	14	15
16	17	18	19	20	21	22
23	24	25	26	27	28	29
30						

"You know, it's really dumb to keep this right next to the cereal. ...
In fact, I don't know why we even keep this stuff around in the first place."

NoVeMBeR 2003

Monday
24

Tuesday
25

Wednesday
26

Thanksgiving (USA)

Thursday
27

Friday
28

Saturday
29

St. Andrew's Day (UK)

Sunday
30

NoVemBer 2003

S	M	T	W	T	F	S
						1
2	3	4	5	6	7	8
9	10	11	12	13	14	15
16	17	18	19	20	21	22
23	24	25	26	27	28	29
30						

"My next guest, on the monitor behind me, is an organized crime informant. To protect his identity, we've placed him in a darkened studio—so let's go to him now."

DeCembeR 2003

Monday

1

Tuesday

2

Wednesday

3

Thursday

4

Friday

5

Saturday

6

DeCembeR 2003

S	M	T	W	T	F	S
	1	2	3	4	5	6
7	8	9	10	11	12	13
14	15	16	17	18	19	20
21	22	23	24	25	26	27
28	29	30	31			

Sunday

7

"I lift, you grab. … Was that concept just a little too complex, Carl?"

DeCembeR 2003

Monday
8

Tuesday
9

Human Rights Day

Wednesday
10

Thursday
11

Friday
12

Saturday
13

Sunday
14

DeCembeR 2003

S	M	T	W	T	F	S
	1	2	3	4	5	6
7	8	9	10	11	12	13
14	15	16	17	18	19	20
21	22	23	24	25	26	27
28	29	30	31			

"Oh, look, this get better ... 'F' in history!
You even flunk something not happen yet?"

DeCembeR 2003

_____
_____
_____
_____
_____
_____
_____
_____
_____
_____
_____
_____
_____
_____
_____
_____
_____
_____
_____
_____
_____
_____

DeCembeR 2003

S	M	T	W	T	F	S
	1	2	3	4	5	6
7	8	9	10	11	12	13
14	15	16	17	18	19	20
21	22	23	24	25	26	27
28	29	30	31			

Monday
15

Tuesday
16

Wednesday
17

Thursday
18

Friday
19

First Day of Hanukkah

Saturday
20

Sunday
21

DeCembeR 2003

Monday
22

Tuesday
23

Christmas Eve

Wednesday
24

Christmas Day

Thursday
25

Kwanzaa begins (USA)
Boxing Day (Canada, NZ, UK, Australia—except SA)
Proclamation Day (Australia—SA)

Friday
26

Last Day of Hanukkah

Saturday
27

Sunday
28

DeCembeR 2003

S	M	T	W	T	F	S
	1	2	3	4	5	6
7	8	9	10	11	12	13
14	15	16	17	18	19	20
21	22	23	24	25	26	27
28	29	30	31			

"You gotta check this out, Stuart. Vinnie's over on the couch putting the move on Zelda Schwartz—but he's talkin' to the wrong end."

DeC 2003-
JAn 2004

Monday
29

Tuesday
30

Wednesday
31

New Year's Day
Kwanzaa ends (USA)

Thursday
1

Day after New Year's Day (NZ)
Bank Holiday (Scotland)

Friday
2

Saturday
3

Sunday
4

JAnUary 2004

S	M	T	W	T	F	S
				1	2	3
4	5	6	7	8	9	10
11	12	13	14	15	16	17
18	19	20	21	22	23	24
25	26	27	28	29	30	31

JANUARY 2004

FEBRUARY 2004

MARCH 2004

APRIL 2004

MAY 2004

JUNE 2004

JuLy 2004

AUguSt 2004

SeptembeR 2004

October 2004

November 2004

December 2004

JANUARY 2002

S	M	T	W	T	F	S
		1	2	3	4	5
6	7	8	9	10	11	12
13	14	15	16	17	18	19
20	21	22	23	24	25	26
27	28	29	30	31		

FebRuary 2002

S	M	T	W	T	F	S
					1	2
3	4	5	6	7	8	9
10	11	12	13	14	15	16
17	18	19	20	21	22	23
24	25	26	27	28		

MArcH 2002

S	M	T	W	T	F	S
					1	2
3	4	5	6	7	8	9
10	11	12	13	14	15	16
17	18	19	20	21	22	23
24/31	25	26	27	28	29	30

ApRil 2002

S	M	T	W	T	F	S
	1	2	3	4	5	6
7	8	9	10	11	12	13
14	15	16	17	18	19	20
21	22	23	24	25	26	27
28	29	30				

May 2002

S	M	T	W	T	F	S
			1	2	3	4
5	6	7	8	9	10	11
12	13	14	15	16	17	18
19	20	21	22	23	24	25
26	27	28	29	30	31	

JuNe 2002

S	M	T	W	T	F	S
						1
2	3	4	5	6	7	8
9	10	11	12	13	14	15
16	17	18	19	20	21	22
23/30	24	25	26	27	28	29

JuLy 2002

S	M	T	W	T	F	S
	1	2	3	4	5	6
7	8	9	10	11	12	13
14	15	16	17	18	19	20
21	22	23	24	25	26	27
28	29	30	31			

AuGuSt 2002

S	M	T	W	T	F	S
				1	2	3
4	5	6	7	8	9	10
11	12	13	14	15	16	17
18	19	20	21	22	23	24
25	26	27	28	29	30	31

SeptembeR 2002

S	M	T	W	T	F	S
1	2	3	4	5	6	7
8	9	10	11	12	13	14
15	16	17	18	19	20	21
22	23	24	25	26	27	28
29	30					

OctobeR 2002

S	M	T	W	T	F	S
		1	2	3	4	5
6	7	8	9	10	11	12
13	14	15	16	17	18	19
20	21	22	23	24	25	26
27	28	29	30	31		

NoVembeR 2002

S	M	T	W	T	F	S
					1	2
3	4	5	6	7	8	9
10	11	12	13	14	15	16
17	18	19	20	21	22	23
24	25	26	27	28	29	30

DeCembeR 2002

S	M	T	W	T	F	S
1	2	3	4	5	6	7
8	9	10	11	12	13	14
15	16	17	18	19	20	21
22	23	24	25	26	27	28
29	30	31				

January 2003

S	M	T	W	T	F	S
			1	2	3	4
5	6	7	8	9	10	11
12	13	14	15	16	17	18
19	20	21	22	23	24	25
26	27	28	29	30	31	

February 2003

S	M	T	W	T	F	S
						1
2	3	4	5	6	7	8
9	10	11	12	13	14	15
16	17	18	19	20	21	22
23	24	25	26	27	28	

March 2003

S	M	T	W	T	F	S
						1
2	3	4	5	6	7	8
9	10	11	12	13	14	15
16	17	18	19	20	21	22
23/30	24/31	25	26	27	28	29

April 2003

S	M	T	W	T	F	S
		1	2	3	4	5
6	7	8	9	10	11	12
13	14	15	16	17	18	19
20	21	22	23	24	25	26
27	28	29	30			

May 2003

S	M	T	W	T	F	S
				1	2	3
4	5	6	7	8	9	10
11	12	13	14	15	16	17
18	19	20	21	22	23	24
25	26	27	28	29	30	31

June 2003

S	M	T	W	T	F	S
1	2	3	4	5	6	7
8	9	10	11	12	13	14
15	16	17	18	19	20	21
22	23	24	25	26	27	28
29	30					

July 2003

S	M	T	W	T	F	S
		1	2	3	4	5
6	7	8	9	10	11	12
13	14	15	16	17	18	19
20	21	22	23	24	25	26
27	28	29	30	31		

August 2003

S	M	T	W	T	F	S
					1	2
3	4	5	6	7	8	9
10	11	12	13	14	15	16
17	18	19	20	21	22	23
24/31	25	26	27	28	29	30

September 2003

S	M	T	W	T	F	S
	1	2	3	4	5	6
7	8	9	10	11	12	13
14	15	16	17	18	19	20
21	22	23	24	25	26	27
28	29	30				

October 2003

S	M	T	W	T	F	S
			1	2	3	4
5	6	7	8	9	10	11
12	13	14	15	16	17	18
19	20	21	22	23	24	25
26	27	28	29	30	31	

November 2003

S	M	T	W	T	F	S
						1
2	3	4	5	6	7	8
9	10	11	12	13	14	15
16	17	18	19	20	21	22
23/30	24	25	26	27	28	29

December 2003

S	M	T	W	T	F	S
	1	2	3	4	5	6
7	8	9	10	11	12	13
14	15	16	17	18	19	20
21	22	23	24	25	26	27
28	29	30	31			

January 2004

S	M	T	W	T	F	S
				1	2	3
4	5	6	7	8	9	10
11	12	13	14	15	16	17
18	19	20	21	22	23	24
25	26	27	28	29	30	31

February 2004

S	M	T	W	T	F	S
1	2	3	4	5	6	7
8	9	10	11	12	13	14
15	16	17	18	19	20	21
22	23	24	25	26	27	28
29						

March 2004

S	M	T	W	T	F	S
	1	2	3	4	5	6
7	8	9	10	11	12	13
14	15	16	17	18	19	20
21	22	23	24	25	26	27
28	29	30	31			

April 2004

S	M	T	W	T	F	S
				1	2	3
4	5	6	7	8	9	10
11	12	13	14	15	16	17
18	19	20	21	22	23	24
25	26	27	28	29	30	

May 2004

S	M	T	W	T	F	S
						1
2	3	4	5	6	7	8
9	10	11	12	13	14	15
16	17	18	19	20	21	22
23/30	24/31	25	26	27	28	29

June 2004

S	M	T	W	T	F	S
		1	2	3	4	5
6	7	8	9	10	11	12
13	14	15	16	17	18	19
20	21	22	23	24	25	26
27	28	29	30			

July 2004

S	M	T	W	T	F	S
				1	2	3
4	5	6	7	8	9	10
11	12	13	14	15	16	17
18	19	20	21	22	23	24
25	26	27	28	29	30	31

August 2004

S	M	T	W	T	F	S
1	2	3	4	5	6	7
8	9	10	11	12	13	14
15	16	17	18	19	20	21
22	23	24	25	26	27	28
29	30	31				

September 2004

S	M	T	W	T	F	S
			1	2	3	4
5	6	7	8	9	10	11
12	13	14	15	16	17	18
19	20	21	22	23	24	25
26	27	28	29	30		

October 2004

S	M	T	W	T	F	S
					1	2
3	4	5	6	7	8	9
10	11	12	13	14	15	16
17	18	19	20	21	22	23
24/31	25	26	27	28	29	30

November 2004

S	M	T	W	T	F	S
	1	2	3	4	5	6
7	8	9	10	11	12	13
14	15	16	17	18	19	20
21	22	23	24	25	26	27
28	29	30				

December 2004

S	M	T	W	T	F	S
			1	2	3	4
5	6	7	8	9	10	11
12	13	14	15	16	17	18
19	20	21	22	23	24	25
26	27	28	29	30	31	

Names and Numbers

Names and Numbers